TEXAS MOTHER GOOSE

By David Davis
Illustrated by Sue Marshall Ward

PELICAN PUBLISHING COMPANY
GRETNA 2012

Text copyright © 2006
By David Davis

Illustrations copyright © 2006
By Sue Marshall Ward
All rights reserved

First printing, August 2006
Second printing, February 2007
Third printing, April 2008
Fourth printing, April 2010
Fifth printing, November 2012

Library of Congress Cataloging-in-Publication Data

Davis, David (David R.), 1948-
  Texas Mother Goose / by David Davis ; illustrated by Sue Marshall Ward.
    p. cm.
  Summary: A Texas twist to classic Mother Goose rhymes with such titles as "Mary Had a White-Faced Calf," "There Was an Old Cowgirl Who Lived in a Boot," and "Pecos Peter, Taco Eater."
  ISBN-13: 978-1-58980-369-5 (hardcover : alk. paper)
  1. Nursery rhymes. 2. Children's poetry.   [1. Nursery rhymes.]
I. Ward, Sue Marshall, 1941-   , ill. II. Mother Goose III. Title.
PZ8.3.D2894Tex 2006
[E]—dc22
                                                      2006004953

Printed in Malaysia
Published by Pelican Publishing Company, Inc.
1000 Burmaster Street, Gretna, Louisiana 70053

Twinkle, Twinkle, Texas Star

Twinkle, twinkle, Texas star,
Above the state where my roots are!
Up above the plains so high,
Lighting up the Lone Star sky.
Twinkle, twinkle, Texas star,
Above the state where my roots are!

When the western sun is gone,
I pat the horse I ride upon.
Cattle sleep in purple night
'Neath your twinkle, twinkle light.
Twinkle, twinkle, Texas star,
Above the state where my roots are!

Your spark's a western twilight lamp
'Round the silent cowboy camp.
I tip my hat to look at you,
Floating in that sky of blue.
A friendly face when I ride far,
Twinkle, twinkle, Texas star.

Texas Mother Goose

When Mother Goose flies to Texas,
She saddles her magic bird,
Wearing cowboy boots and silver spurs,
With twinkling stars to herd.
Out of the Texas sky she glides,
To children down below;
Circling past the cotton clouds,
She lands near the Alamo.
So, gather 'round the campfire,
Little partners brave and true.
Rest your ponies for the night;
She's got Texas rhymes for you.

Jumping Jack

Jack jump high; Jack jump higher,
Over the mesquite cooking fire.
He jumped too low and burned his tail
And had to sit in the water pail.

Cowpoke Georgie

Cowpoke Georgie, sweet pecan pie,
Kissed cowgirls and made them sigh;
More cowboys came riding through,
Ran him off, and kissed them too.

Yankee Doodle Moved Out West

Yankee Doodle moved out West,
Riding on a stallion.
He bought a Texas cowboy hat;
He'd wanted a "ten gallon."

Texas Prayer

By the campfire, 'bout to sleep,
I pray the Lord my soul to keep.
Wake me early, wake me late,
But let me rise in the Lone Star State.

Hickety, Pickety, My Border Collie

Hickety, pickety, my border collie
Herds the cattle each day, by golly;
Cowpokes ride from far away
To watch my cow dog work and play.
His reward's a pat from Molly,
Hickety, pickety, my border collie.

Hush Little Young'un

Hush, little young'un, don't you squall;
Papa's gonna teach you the Texas drawl.
If that Texas drawl won't sing,
Papa's gonna buy you a silver ring.
If that silver ring must sell,
Daddy's gonna buy you an oil well.
If that oil well runs dry,
Papa's gonna buy you a summer sky.
If that summer sky's not blue,
Papa's gonna whisper, "I love you."

Hill Country Baby

Hill country baby, hear whippoorwills,
On the hill crest, the evening is still;
When nighttime falls, we'll both stroll inside,
To your cedar cradle that rocks by my side.

On Lacy's Farm

In the piney woods near Lacy's farm,
A blue jay perched on Bennie's arm.
Margie knew just what to do:
She stirred up cocoa milk for two.
The blue jay asked, "Where's some for me?"
And waited in the sweet gum tree.
In their red wagon, off they wheeled,
To buy milk in New Summerfield.
At ten o'clock, or just before,
They climbed the steps to Tipton's store
And counted dimes so they could say,
"Milk for us—and one blue jay."

Sleepy Little Buckaroo

Sleepy little buckaroo,
You had a busy day.
On your stick horse,
You rode the range
And watched the dogies play.
Close your eyes
And rest tonight;
There's no need for sorrow.
You'll wake to greet the Texas sun
And ride the trail tomorrow.

There Was an Old Cowgirl Who Lived in a Boot

There was an old cowgirl who lived in a boot;
She had so many young'uns, she wanted to scoot.
"We're needing bedrooms!" they yodeled at her;
So she added on a bright-silver spur.

Gulf of Mexico

At the Gulf of Mexico,
I shift sand with my big toe.
I ride the waves for summer fun
And build sandcastles in the sun.

Five Macho Vaqueros

Five macho vaqueros
Wore big sombreros
While strutting in the square.
But little Luis
Walked a mouse on a leash
And suddenly no one was there.

Silver Saddles

Silver saddles in the sun,
Wish that I was riding one.
The Conchos shines
With sparkly gleams
In every little cowpoke's dreams.

The Bells of Mission San Jose

The bells of Mission San Jose
Call me when I'm far away;
I'll return to my Texas home
And mission bells of San Antone.

Song of Texas

Sing a song of Texas,
Bluebonnets ankle-high;
Four and twenty mockingbirds
Circle in the sky.

When the sky turned sunny,
The birds began to sing;
Isn't that a pretty song
For Texas in the spring?

Pretty Maria

Pat-a-cake, pat-a-cake, pretty Maria,
Pat out the dough to make a tortilla.
Roll it and cook it, all flat and round,
And eat it for dinner in old Fort Worth town.

Watermelon

Red and green,
Now children see
Watermelon
For you and me.
Suck the juice and spit the seeds;
That's all a Texas young'un needs.

Pecos Peter, Taco Eater

Pecos Peter, taco eater,
Married a gal and couldn't keep her;
He put her in a taco shell,
And there he kept her, I heard tell.

Pecos Peter, taco eater,
Had another and didn't love her;
He ate up all the taco shells
And rode his horse to Mineral Wells.

Sand Hill Jack

Sand Hill Jack could eat no fat;
His wife could eat no lean;
So he ate fresh okra stew,
And she, cornbread and beans.

Mary, Mary, from Old Granbury

Mary, Mary, from old Granbury,
How does your garden grow?
With black-eyed peas and honeybees,
It's quite a row to hoe.

This is the Barn That Zeke Built

This is the barn that Zeke built.
This is the corn
That spilled in the barn that Zeke built.
This is the pig
That gobbled the corn
That spilled in the barn that Zeke built.
This is the dog
That snapped at the pig
That gobbled the corn
That spilled in the barn that Zeke built.
This is the cat
That hissed at the dog
That snapped at the pig
That gobbled the corn
That spilled in the barn that Zeke built.
This is the rat
That ran from the cat
That hissed at the dog
That snapped at the pig
That gobbled the corn
That spilled in the barn that Zeke built.
This is the maiden who yelled "Eek!" at the rat
That ran from the cat
That hissed at the dog
That snapped at the pig
That gobbled the corn
That spilled in the barn that Zeke built.
This is the cowboy long and tall
Who kissed the maiden who yelled, "Eek!" at the rat
That ran from the cat
That hissed at the dog

That snapped at the pig
That gobbled the corn
That spilled in the barn that Zeke built.
This is the goat with curling horns
That butted the cowboy long and tall
Who kissed the maiden who yelled "Eek!" at the rat
That ran from the cat
That hissed at the dog
That snapped at the pig
That gobbled the corn
That spilled in the barn that Zeke built.
This is the farmhand all handsome and strong
Who belled the goat with curling horns
That butted the cowboy long and tall
Who kissed the maiden who yelled "Eek!" at the rat
That ran from the cat
That hissed at the dog
That snapped at the pig
That gobbled the corn
That spilled in the barn that Zeke built.
This is the rooster that crowed loud at sunrise,
That waked the farmhand all handsome and strong
Who belled the goat with the curling horns
That butted the cowboy long and tall
Who kissed the maiden who yelled "Eek!" at the rat
That ran from the cat
That hissed at the dog
That snapped at the pig
That gobbled the corn
That spilled in the barn that Zeke built.

Winkin', Blinkin', and Nod

Winkin', Blinkin', and Nod, one night, rode the
   range in a cowboy boot.
They crossed the crystal Milky Way seeking
   nighttime cowpoke loot.
"Where are you boys heading; what do you hanker
   for?" asked the big old Texas moon.
"We've a mind to gather maverick stars this
   Lone Star night in June."
"Lariats of silver and gold have we," said
   Winkin', Blinkin', and Nod.
"Twirl your ropes wherever you will," said the
   capering milky stars.
"But you won't put your brand on us," they
   laughed as they galloped the sky past Mars.
So cried the stars to the cowboy three—Winkin',
   Blinkin', and Nod.
The old moon laughed and yodeled a tune as
   they listened to every word,
And they lassoed stars in the fluffy clouds till
   they gathered a heavenly herd.

Then downward flew the hand-tooled boot
  from the roundup in the sky.
Some folks claim it's a dream they had, like all
  dreamers by and by,
But I shall name these cowboys three, Winkin',
  Blinkin', and Nod.
Now, Winkin' and Blinkin' are two little eyes,
  and Nod is a little head,
And the cowboy boot that rode the range is a
  bunkhouse baby's bed.
So, rest your eyes while Mama sings of
  the wonderful sights you'll see,
And you'll ride the dewy, misty plains
  with those western cowboys three—
    Winkin', Blinkin', and Nod.

Hey, Diddle Diddle

Hey, diddle diddle,
The cat and the fiddle,
The cows sang at Lukenbach.
They became country stars with
Cadillac cars,
And the farmer was quite rightly
shocked.

Indian Babies

Long ago, down Blanco way,
Indian babies loved to play
By singing springs in the Texas dawn;
Where have all those babies gone?

Good Old Neb Was a Whittling Fool

Good old Neb was a whittling fool.
He carved a cane, and he whittled a stool;
Neb whittled a collar for his old hound dog,
Then he hollowed a house from an old oak log.
Just when we thought his work was through,
He whittled wood whistles for me and you.

Polly, Drop the Ice Cubes In

Polly, drop the ice cubes in,
Polly, drop the ice cubes in,
Polly, drop the ice cubes in,
We'll have iced tea.
Johnny, take them out again,
Johnny, take them out again,
Johnny, take them out again,
Our kin's gone away.

Little Miss Toni

Little Miss Toni
Sat on her pony,
Eating her biscuit and jerky;
Along came a bee,
Which perched on her knee,
And she flew through the air
Like a turkey.

Hickory, Dickory, Dock

Hickory, dickory, dock,
A bull charged up the clock.
He smashed it flat,
And that was that,
Hickory, dickory, dock.

Cactus Jack Horner

Cactus Jack Horner
Held a bowl in the corner,
With a grin on his face that looked silly;
He dipped in a spoon
And started to swoon
Then said, "Who put beans in my chili?"

Breakfast with Humpty Dumpty

Humpty Dumpty sat on a wall.
Humpty Dumpty had a great fall.
All the ranch cowboys and all the vaqueros
Got a big breakfast of huevos rancheros.

Billy Joseph Angus Pratt

Billy Joseph Angus Pratt
Napped in daddy's cowboy hat.
He put a pillow inside the brim;
There was room for teddy, dog, and him.

Three Armadillos

On three silky pillows
Sat three armadillos
Eating cakes and tea;
They gobble so fast,
The vittles won't last;
Will they save a bite for me?

Merchant Molly

Merchant Molly munched a tamale
While shopping at the *mercado*.
She bought enchiladas
And two empanadas
And bright emerald green avocados.
They fried papas fritas
For this sweet señorita;
And this little girl was a winner.
She picked a pequeño chili relleno
To fill up her tummy till dinner.

Austin Song

A Texas senator said to me,
"I'm looking for a meal that's free."
The governor stated, passing through,
"If he gets one, will you buy mine too?"

Rub-a-Dub-Dub

Rub-a-dub-dub,
Three men in a tub
Took a bath—what a sight to see!
A mud-covered dude
Asked in a manner quite rude,
"Is there room for my horse and me?"

What Are Little Cowboys Made Of?

What are little cowboys made of?
Spurs and chaps
And ten-gallon hats,
And that's what little cowboys are made of.

What Are Little Cowgirls Made Of?

What are little cowgirls made of?
Bluebonnets and spring
And notes songbirds sing,
And that's what little cowgirls are made of.

Sidesaddle Sue

Sidesaddle Sue loves barbecue,
And she rises 'fore the sun's first ray.
And Sue calls for the meat
And mesquite wood for heat,
Then she cooks all through the day.
Sue heaps the plates sharp at eight,
And a very fine feed has she.
Eat some grub quick till you're full as a tick
With pinto beans and coleslaw greens,
A feast for you and me.

West Texas Willy

West Texas Willy runs through town,
Wearing stovepipe boots and his shirttail down,
Knocking on the windows, yelling every night,
"Have you traveled west at twilight and seen the Marfa lights?"

Little Buckaroo

"Little buckaroo,
Come and throw your rope.
There're hogs in the melons;
Our herd's down the slope.
And where is the cowhand
Who watches our cattle?"
"Asleep by a cactus,
With his head on his saddle."
"You fixin' to wake him?"
"No, pard', not me!
He'd pitch such a fit,
I'll just let him be."

Sweet Josephina

Sweet Josephina
Had a pet javelina
That loved to run and play.
And I hear tell,
He wore a bell
That tinkled all the day.

Padre Pedro Picked a Passel of Peppers on the Pedernales

Padre Pedro picked a passel of peppers on the Pedernales.
A passel of Pedernales peppers Padre Pedro picked.
If Padre Pedro picked a passel of Pedernales peppers,
Where's the passel of Pedernales peppers Padre Pedro picked?

Come with Me to the Old State Fair

Come with me to the old state fair
And hear Big Tex say, "Howdy there."
Watch the barkers bark, see the champion hog,
While you take a bite from a fat corn dog.

Chili

Chili peppers hot,
Chili peppers cold,
Hot chili in the pot
Nine days old.
Some like it hot,
Some like it cold,
Some like it in the pot
Nine days old.

Jack and Jill

Jack and Jill scurried up the hill
To drill a well for water.
Jack fell joggin' and bumped his noggin,
And Jill came tumbling after.

Up they got and home did trot,
Rewarded for their toil:
They were coated head to toe in black,
For the children had struck oil.

Mary Had a White-Faced Calf

Mary had a white-faced calf
Too young to eat sweet hay,
So she fed him from a bottle,
And he followed her all day.

Three Blind Mice

Three blind mice,
See how they run!
They ran for Senate up Austin way,
Since they're blind it's the place to stay;
They're just like senators in every way,
Those three blind mice.

Get Your Fiddle

Get your fiddle,
Start to sing,
Papa's playing
Texas swing.
Strum guitars,
Tap your toes,
Dance all night,
Sweet Texas Rose.

The Taco Man

Oh, do you know the taco man,
With the frying pan, at the taco stand?
Oh, do you know the taco man?
I'm hungry, I must say!

Oh, yes, I know the taco man,
With the frying pan, at the taco stand;
Oh, yes, I know the taco man,
Down Corpus Christi way.